SUPER ANIMAL ADVENTURE SQUAD

Hush-hush

TOP SECRET!

NO PEEKING!

SUPER ANIMAL ADVENTURE SQUAD
A DAVID FICKLING BOOK 978 1 849 92172 5

First published thanks to the amazing DFC weekly comic,
May 2008 – March 2009

Published in Great Britain in 2011 by David Fickling Books,
a division of Random House Children's Publishers UK
A Random House Group Company
This edition published 2013

1 3 5 7 9 10 8 6 4 2

Copyright © James Turner 2011

DAVID FICKLING BOOKS 31 Beaumont Street, Oxford, OX1 2NP

www.randomhousechildrens.co.uk
www.randomhouse.co.uk

Addresses for companies within The Random House Group Limited can be found at:
www.randomhouse.co.uk/offices.htm

THE RANDOM HOUSE GROUP Limited Reg. No. 954009

A CIP catalogue record for this book is available from the British Library.
Printed in China

The Random House Group Limited supports the Forest Stewardship Council® (FSC®),
the leading international forest-certification organisation. Our books carrying the FSC
label are printed on FSC®-certified paper. FSC is the only forest-certification scheme
supported by the leading environmental organisations, including Greenpeace.
Our paper procurement policy can be found at
www.randomhouse.co.uk/environment

MIX
Paper from
responsible sources
FSC
www.fsc.org
FSC® C104723

FOR MY JADE BABOON

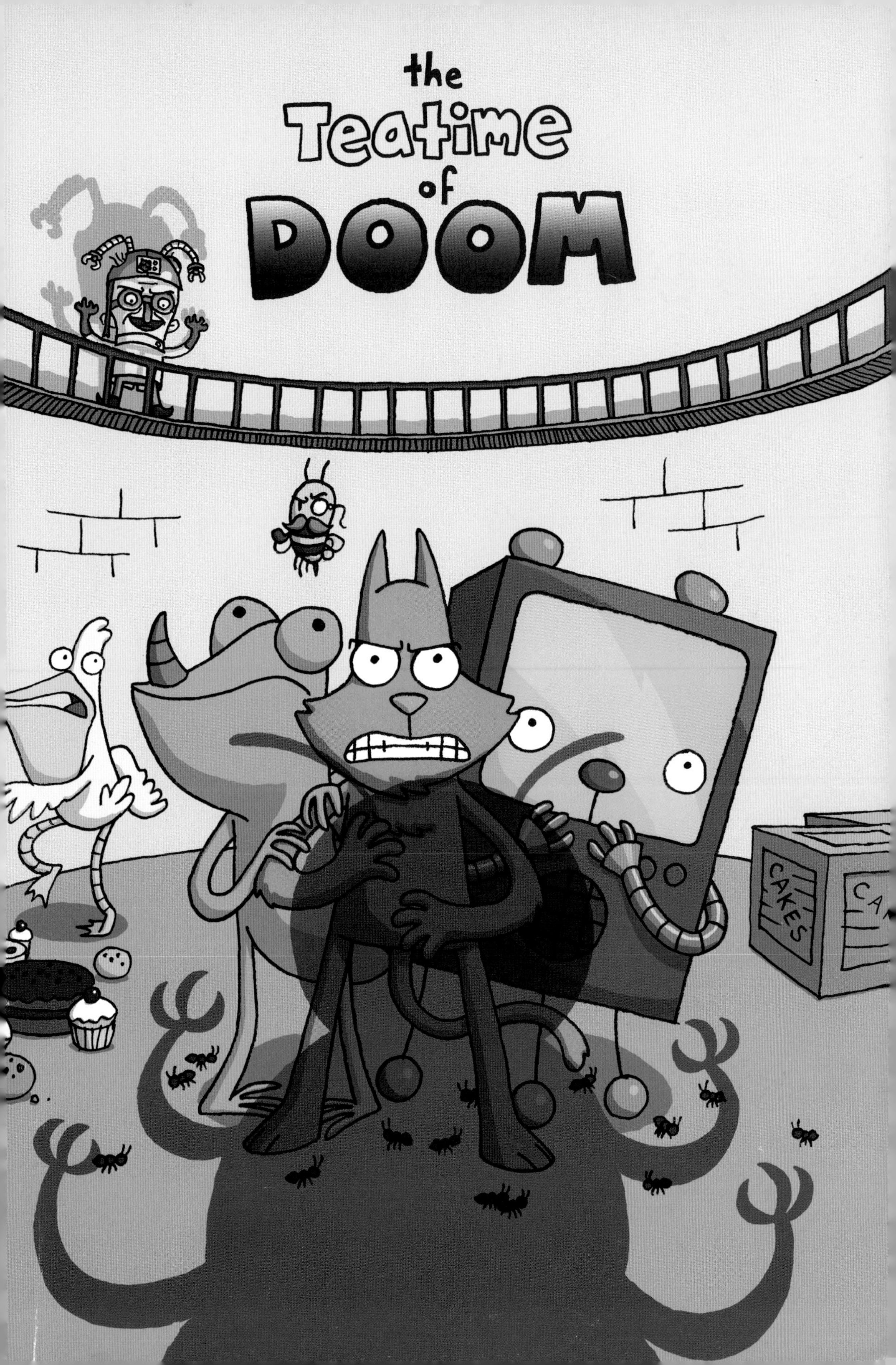
the Teatime of DOOM
CAKES
CAKES

SUPER ANIMAL ADVENTURE SQUAD

IN:
THE TEATIME OF DOOM
PART ONE
BY JAMES TURNER

ONE DAY, IN A QUIET LOCAL BAKERY...

OOH, I THINK I'LL TAKE A SLICE OF THAT TASTY LOOKING CHOCOLATE CAKE, PLEASE, MR CRUMBLE.

CERTAINLY, MRS BICYCLE!

BUT!

WELL THAT'S A LITTLE UNUSUAL...!

HOP!

CHOP!

MY CAKES! SOMEBODY STOP MY CAKES!

OH MY! PERHAPS IT'S TIME I WENT ON A DIET.

FORTUNATELY, IN A SECURE GOVERNMENT FACILITY, A TEAM OF ELITE AGENTS IS EVER ALERT TO THE CALL TO ACTION...

Yeastenders

ZZZ

AGENT K! AGENT K! COME IN!

THIS IS A LEVEL 6 CAKE EMERGENCY!

AGENT K REPORTING, SIR! WHAT VILLAINY IS AFOOT?

SALUTE!

VILLAINY OF THE WORST SORT!...

CAKES AND PASTRIES OF ALL KINDS HAVE BEEN ESCAPING FROM BAKERIES ALL OVER THE COUNTRY!

CAKES   ICING
SPONGE   TASTY STUFF
BUNS   NICE THINGS
NUM   OH BOY!

IF THEY CAN'T BE RECOVERED BY TEATIME, I DREAD TO THINK WHAT MIGHT HAPPEN!

FLAMING FAIRYCAKES! WITHOUT A MID-AFTERNOON TREAT THE VERY ICING OF SOCIETY WOULD DISSOLVE! WE'LL BEGIN THE SEARCH AT ONCE!

GOOD LUCK, AGENT. OVER AND OUT!

IT'S TIME FOR ACTION, AGENTS! THE FATE OF CIVILIZATION AS WE KNOW IT IS AT STAKE!

DO I HAVE TIME TO MAKE A SANDWICH FIRST?

AGENT REX

AGENT IRWIN

I SAY, ANOTHER ADVENTURE! HOW SPIFFING!

WHAT'S THE MISSION THIS TIME, AGENT K?

AGENT BEESLEY

CLANK

WHIRR

AGENT BEARBOT

IT'S OUR MOST VITAL MISSION YET, AGENTS..

AW, I WAS WATCHING THAT!

IT'S UP TO US TO PREVENT...
THE TEATIME OF DOOM!

DOES ANYONE KNOW HOW TO SET THE TIVO?

BY JOVE!

YIKES! CAN THEY DO IT?

SUPER ANIMAL ADVENTURE SQUAD

BY JAMES TURNER

IN: THE TEATIME OF DOOM PART TWO

CAKES ARE DISAPPEARING ALL ACROSS THE COUNTRY, AND IT'S UP TO THE SUPER ANIMAL ADVENTURE SQUAD TO FIND OUT WHO'S BEHIND IT - IN TIME TO STOP ...THE TEATIME OF DOOM!

QUICKLY AGENTS, TO THE SUPER ADVENTURE MOBILE!

OOH - WE HAVE A MOBILE?

...

WORDS DO NOT EXIST TO SUFFICIENTLY EXPRESS MY DISAPPOINTMENT.

KEEP YOUR EYES PEELED FOR ANY SIGNS OF CAKE ACTIVITY, AGENTS!

HEE HEE! FROM UP HERE THE PEOPLE LOOK LIKE ANTS!

THOSE ARE ANTS, REX. WE HAVEN'T TAKEN OFF YET.

OHHH.

AND LOOK! THE DIMINUTIVE DEVILS HAVE THE CAKES!

QUICKLY! LET'S GAIN SOME HEIGHT AND FIND OUT WHERE THEY'RE TAKING THEM!

IT LOOKS LIKE THEY'RE ALL HEADED FOR THE OLD ABANDONED OBSERVATORY. TAKE US DOWN NICE AND SLOW, AGENT REX ...

AYE-AYE CAPTAIN!

BUT WHAT MANNER OF VILLAIN AWAITS INSIDE? IT IS NONE OTHER THAN THE WORLD'S MADDEST MAD SCIENTIST, DOCTOR NEFARIOUS!

YES! YES! MY INSECT CONTROL HELMET IS A SUCCESS! SOON MY PLAN WILL BE COMPLETE!

NO ONE CAN STOP ME NOW!

NO ONE BUT —

CRASH!

THE SUPER ANIMAL ADVENTURE SQUAD! NO!

PFFT

I DO WISH THEY'D USE THE FRONT DOOR FOR A CHANGE.

WILL OUR HEROES RECOVER THE CAKES IN TIME?

SUPER ANIMAL ADVENTURE SQUAD

BY JAMES TURNER

IN: **THE TEATIME OF DOOM** PART THREE

IN PURSUIT OF AN ARMY OF CAKE-STEALING ANTS OUR HEROES HAVE CRASHED THROUGH THE ROOF OF AN OBSERVATORY AND DISCOVERED THE VILLAIN BEHIND THE SCHEME...

DOCTOR NEFARIOUS! I SHOULD HAVE KNOWN YOU'D BE BEHIND THE SCHEME! WHAT VILLAINY ARE YOU UP TO THIS TIME?

AND WHY ARE YOU WEARING SUCH A SILLY HAT?

I'M BLIND!

DUST

DUST

IT IS A PLAN AS SIMPLE AS IT IS INGENIOUS:

WITH THIS INSECT CONTROL HELMET I CAN COMMAND EVERY ANT IN THE WORLD!

SMUG

ONCE MY INSECT SLAVES HAVE COLLECTED EVERY CAKE ON THE PLANET, THE PEOPLE WILL BE POWERLESS...

...POWERLESS TO RESIST MY DELICIOUS NEFARIOUS BRAND SPONGE CAKES™! MADE WITH REAL BROCCOLI!

UGH- BUT THESE ARE REVOLTING!

NEFARIOUS SPONGECAKES SO TASTY!

CHEW

CHEW

CAKES

BUT SINCE I CONTROL EVERY CAKE IN THE WORLD, WHAT CHOICE WILL PEOPLE HAVE?

UGH NOM NOM UGH

TEATIME WILL BE MINE TO RULE AS I WISH! HA HA HA HA HA HA!

YOU FIEND! YOU WON'T GET AWAY WITH THIS!

AGENTS! IT'S TIME FOR ACTION!

FOOLS! YOU CAN'T STOP ME... NOT WHEN I HAVE AN ARMY OF ANTS AT MY COMMAND!

GET THEM, MY MANY-LEGGED MINIONS!

CAKES

CAKES

HMM...I THINK THIS CALLS FOR PLAN OMEGA THETA...

OOH - THAT'S MY FAVOURITE PLAN!

I'LL FETCH THE DUCK AND THE CRASH HELMET!

THIS WAY!

NO REX, PLAN OMEGA THETA IS WHERE YOU AND I KEEP THE DOCTOR BUSY WHILE THE REST OF THE SQUAD CLIMBS ONTO THAT GANTRY AND TRIES TO SNEAK AROUND BEHIND HIM.

GANTRY 7

OH.

YOU'RE THINKING OF PLAN OMEGA ALPHA.

AND SO!

GOOD LUCK, CHAPS!

I WISH I HADN'T EATEN ALL THOSE CAKES...

BLOIK

WAK?

GRR

HISS!

HOW WILL OUR HEROES GET OUT OF THIS STICKY SITUATION?

SUPER ANIMAL ADVENTURE SQUAD

BY JAMES TURNER

IN: THE TEATIME OF DOOM — PART FOUR

WHILE TRYING TO RECOVER THE NATION'S STOLEN CAKES, TWO OF OUR HEROES HAVE BEEN SURROUNDED BY THE ANT SLAVES OF THE EVIL DR NEFARIOUS. CAN THE REST OF THE SQUAD SAVE THEM IN TIME?

AAAAH! THEY'RE ON ME! THEY'RE ON ME!

REX, THEY'RE JUST ANTS. THEY CAN'T ACTUALLY HURT YOU.

I KNOW, BUT THEY'RE SO TICKLY!

SCRITCH!

SCRATCH!

I THINK THEY MIGHT NEED A LITTLE HELP.

SO CHAPS, WHAT'S THE PLAN?

FIND MORE CAKES?

WU HA HA HA!

OH! AH!

IT TICKLES!

I CALCULATE THAT A SUFFICIENTLY MASSIVE OBJECT, ACCELERATED UNDER GRAVITY FROM THIS ELEVATION, WOULD DELIVER A SUFFICIENT TRANSFER OF KINETIC ENERGY TO DISABLE HIS CRANIALLY MOUNTED CONTROL DEVICE!

EH?

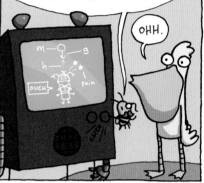

I BELIEVE WHAT OUR ELECTRONIC COMPANION IS TRYING TO SAY IS: 'IF WE DROP SOMETHING ON HIS HEAD, WE CAN BREAK HIS HAT'.

OHH.

m—O——g

h

OUCH

pain

PRECISELY — WE MUST SELECT SOMETHING THAT WILL STRIKE WITH THE MINIMUM FORCE REQUIRED TO DISABLE THE HELMET WITHOUT HURTING ANYONE BELOW — IT'S AN EXTREMELY DELICATE OPERATION...

I THINK I MIGHT HAVE AN IDEA...

I SAY.

SHOVE!

THIS IS NOT EXACTLY WHAT I HAD IN MIIIIIIIIIND!

BY JOVE! SPIFFING WORK, IRWIN! YOU KNOCKED THE BLIGHTER OUT COLD AND SMASHED HIS HELMET TO BOOT!

CHOM CHOM

I DID? UH, I MEAN YES, THAT IS EXACTLY WHAT I MEANT TO DO.

YES! VICTORY IS MINE!

I CAN'T IMAGINE ANY WAY I CAN BE DEFEATED NOW!...

CRUNCH!

SYNTAX ERROR!

OI!

OUCH

HAVE THE SUPER ANIMAL ADVENTURE SQUAD SAVED THE DAY?

SUPER ANIMAL ADVENTURE SQUAD

BY JAMES TURNER

IN: THE TEATIME OF DOOM — PART FIVE

THE SQUAD HAS SUCCESSFULLY FOILED DOCTOR NEFARIOUS' PLAN TO USE ANTS TO STEAL THE WORLD'S CAKES AND FORCE PEOPLE TO BUY HIS DISGUSTING BROCCOLI SPONGES. TEATIME IS SAVED! OR IS IT?...

THE ANTS! WITH THE DOCTOR'S INSECT-CONTROL HELMET DESTROYED, THEY'VE STOPPED TICKLING US!

WE'RE SAVED!

AW — I WAS JUST STARTING TO ENJOY THAT...

AGENT BEARBOT? ARE YOU ALRIGHT?

DON'T WORRY ABOUT ME, SIR — MY FUTURISTIC HYPER-ALLOY SHELL IS QUITE INDESTRUCTIBLE.

GROAN...

COULD YOU PASS ME MY ARM?

I'M 100% SELF REPAIRING, TOO — SEE, AS GOOD AS NEW!

OOPS! SORRY! BUTTERFINGERS!

CRASH

WHAT WILL WE DO WITH DR NEFARIOUS?

DON'T WORRY, AGENT REX...

NO! NO! STAY BACK, I SAY! STAY BAAACK!

...WITHOUT HIS HELMET TO CONTROL THEM, THE ANTS HAVE TURNED ON THEIR MASTER.

HISS

GRR

YOU'RE FREE NOW, GENTLE INSECTS, FREE FROM THE TINY ANT-SIZED YOKE OF TYRANNY!

GO NOW, AND LIVE OUT THE REST OF YOUR SIMPLE LIVES IN PEACE.

OH!

AAH!

HEE HEE!

NOO!

I HAVE ANTS IN MY PANTS!

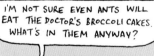

WOO

YAY

HEY! WHAT DID I MISS?

IRWIN! THE ANTS!

FLAP!

SQUDGE

SQUODGE

EW — WELL THEY SHOULDN'T HAVE BEEN LYING AROUND ON THE FLOOR...

SORRY WE STEPPED ON YOUR FRIENDS, LITTLE FELLER. HAVE SOME CAKE TO CHEER YOU UP!

YUM.

I'M NOT SURE EVEN ANTS WILL EAT THE DOCTOR'S BROCCOLI CAKES. WHAT'S IN THEM ANYWAY?

NOM NOM NOM.

INGREDIENTS: SUGAR, SALT, BROCCOLI, FLOUR, BROCCOLI EXTRACT, PARTIALLY INVERTED BROCCOLI OIL, SODIUM TRI-SULPHATE AND ANT MUTAGEN X-13.

IT'S SHOCKING WHAT THEY'LL PUT IN CAKES THESE DAYS.

BURP

WAIT... WHAT WAS THAT LAST ONE AGAIN?

GROW!

MUTATE!

UH OH! ARE THE SQUAD ABOUT TO BECOME ANT FOOD?

SUPER ANIMAL ADVENTURE SQUAD

BY JAMES TURNER

IN: THE TEATIME OF DOOM PART SIX

AFTER FOILING A MAD SCIENTIST'S PLAN TO STEAL EVERY CAKE IN THE WORLD, OUR HEROES HAVE BECOME TRAPPED IN AN OLD ABANDONED OBSERVATORY WITH A GIGANTIC MUTATED ANT!

THIS COULD BE PROBLEMATIC.

MAYBE IT'S A FRIENDLY GIANT MUTANT ANT?

GRRRRRR...

OR POSSIBLY NOT...

GRAAAA!

THWACK!

CRASH!

QUICKLY, AGENTS! TAKE COVER BEHIND THESE CRATES!

GRAAA!

CAKES

ALRIGHT, IT LOOKS LIKE WE'RE SAFE FOR NOW, BUT WE'D BETTER COME UP WITH A PLAN... HOW CAN WE BEAT A GIANT ANT?

?

UM - WE COULD SQUASH IT WITH AN ENORMOUS SHOE?

TOO IMPRACTICAL.

OH, I KNOW! WE COULD GET A REALLY BIG ANTEATER TO EAT IT!

YUM YUM!

TOO IMPOSSIBLE.

WE COULD DISTRACT IT WITH THE WORLD'S BIGGEST PICNIC?

OH BOY!

WHERE WOULD WE GET THAT MUCH SALAD CREAM?

OR HOW ABOUT I LET THE BLIGHTER SWALLOW ME AND I'LL BLOW IT TO SMITHEREENS FROM THE INSIDE! HA!

DYNAMITE

I...LET'S KEEP THAT AS A BACKUP PLAN, BEESLEY.

IT'S NO GOOD - NONE OF THESE PLANS WILL DO. THERE MUST BE SOMETHING WE'RE NOT THINKING OF...

GLI...

I THOUGHT MY IDEA WAS JOLLY GOOD...

BEESLEY, THAT'S IT! YOUR MONOCLE! WE'LL FOCUS THE SUN'S RAYS WITH A GIANT MAGNIFYING GLASS AND USE IT TO BLAST THE ANT!

I SAY! WHAT A DASHED CLEVER PLAN!

SINGE!

BUT WHERE ARE WE GOING TO FIND A LENS BIG ENOUGH IN AN OBSERVATORY?

GIANT TELESCOPE

TOP A GO

CAUTION: REALLY BIG LENS

KEEP READING!

SUPER ANIMAL ADVENTURE SQUAD

BY JAMES TURNER

IN: THE TEATIME OF DOOM — PART SEVEN

TRAPPED IN AN OBSERVATORY WITH A GIGANTIC MUTATED ANT, OUR HEROES HAVE COME UP WITH A PLAN TO USE THE LENS FROM THE TELESCOPE TO FOCUS THE SUN'S RAYS AND DESTROY THE BEAST...

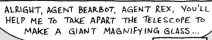

ALRIGHT, AGENT BEARBOT, AGENT REX, YOU'LL HELP ME TO TAKE APART THE TELESCOPE TO MAKE A GIANT MAGNIFYING GLASS...

GIANT TELESCOPE

YES, SIR!

SOUNDS LIKE A GOOD PLAN!

IRWIN, BEESLEY, YOU'LL KEEP THE GIANT ANT BUSY WHILE WE WORK.

I SAY! WHAT FUN!

ON SECOND THOUGHTS, PERHAPS WE SHOULD RETHINK THIS...

GOOD LUCK, AGENTS — YOU'LL NEED IT.

YOU CAN JOLLY WELL COUNT ON US, SIR!

M-MAYBE THE ANT'S GIVEN UP AND GONE HOME?

OR MAYBE NOT...

GRRRR

OH DEAR.

MUMMY!

WARNING THIS IS A DEAD-END DO NOT RUN INTO IT WHEN BEING CHASED BY GIANT ANTS

UH-OH!

SKID!

LOOK, IF THIS IS ABOUT ME STEPPING ON THOSE OTHER ANTS, THAT REALLY WAS AN ACCIDENT...

GRRRR...

IT WON'T HAPPEN AGAIN, I PROMISE!

...

CRUNCH

WELL, I DON'T THINK I CAN BE HELD ENTIRELY RESPONSIBLE FOR THAT.

I REALLY HOPE THEY'VE ALMOST FINISHED MAKING THAT MAGNIFYING GLASS...

GULP.

GRRRR...

MEANWHILE... "TO REMOVE THE LENS, FIRST UNDO THE SCREWS NUMBERED 12 TO 134..."

WOULD NOW BE A BAD TIME TO MENTION THAT I JUST SWALLOWED THE SCREWDRIVER?

IS IRWIN DOOMED?

★ SUPER ★ ANIMAL ADVENTURE SQUAD

BY JAMES TURNER

IN: **THE TEATIME OF DOOM** PART EIGHT

IRWIN AND BEESLEY ARE BATTLING A GIGANTIC MUTATED ANT WHILE THE REST OF THE SQUAD RUSHES TO BUILD A GIANT MAGNIFYING GLASS WITH WHICH TO DEFEAT IT!

GRRRRRRR...

M-MAYBE WE COULD TALK ABOUT THIS?

?

I SAY, OLD CHAP, HOW ABOUT PICKING ON SOMEONE YOUR OWN SIZE?

TAP! TAP!

BEESLEY!

NOW SEE HERE, WHAT'S THE NEED FOR ALL THIS KERFUFFLE?

POUR!

HOW ABOUT WE DISCUSS THIS OVER A NICE CUP OF TEA, LIKE GENTLEMEN.

GRAAA!

SWIPE!

·SMASH!·

RIGHT, THAT'S HOW IT'S GOING TO BE, IS IT? THEN LET'S SETTLE THIS INSECT TO INSECT!

PREPARE YOURSELF FOR A SOUND THRASHING!

TAKE THAT! AND THAT!

PIF! PAF!

AND ALSO A PORTION OF THIS!

GRAB!

SO, HAD ENOUGH, EH? VERY WELL, I ACCEPT YOUR SURRENDER.

HOOK!

I SAY.

COME BACK HERE, YOU COWARD!

YANK!

GRAAAA!

WHY THE DEUCE DID YOU BRING ME UP HERE? I HAD THE BRUTE RIGHT WHERE I WANTED HIM!

WIND WIND

THERE'S NO NEED TO WORRY ABOUT THAT NOW, BEESLEY...

...THE GIANT MAGNIFYING GLASS IS READY!

BY JOVE!

CAN I GET DOWN NOW?

...

AND THEY SAID MY SHOE IDEA WAS NO GOOD...

WILL THE SQUAD'S PLAN REALLY WORK?

SUPER ANIMAL ADVENTURE SQUAD

BY JAMES TURNER

IN: **THE TEATIME OF DOOM** PART NINE

TRAPPED IN AN ABANDONED OBSERVATORY WITH A GIGANTIC MUTATED ANT, OUR HEROES HAVE BUILT A GIANT MAGNIFYING GLASS WITH WHICH TO DEFEAT THE BEAST...

ALRIGHT, SQUAD, THE GIANT MAGNIFYING GLASS IS IN POSITION...

...BUT HOW ARE WE GOING TO LURE THE ANT INTO THE RIGHT SPOT?

HEY, GUYS! COME QUICK!

LEAPING LENSES!

WHAT IS IT, REX??

MY HAND LOOKS HUGE UNDER THIS THING! CHECK IT OUT!

...THAT GIVES ME AN IDEA...

SO...

FREE ANT FOOD ↓

HEE HEE! THIS IS A FUN GAME!

OH, HELLO!

FREE ANT FOOD ↓

GRRRRR...

SNIFF

SNIFF

HA HA! THAT TICKLES!

STEP

THE TARGET IS IN POSITION!

FIRE!

GRUAAAA!

FOCUS!

SHINE!

IT'S WORKING! IT'S WORKING!

OH DEAR... I REALLY SHOULD HAVE READ THE WEATHER FORECAST THIS MORNING...

OVER-CAST!

EXTREME ANT FURY

IS THIS THE END FOR OUR HEROES? TURN OVER TO FIND OUT!

SUPER ANIMAL ADVENTURE SQUAD

BY JAMES TURNER

IN: **THE TEATIME OF DOOM** PART TEN

TRAPPED IN AN OBSERVATORY WITH A GIGANTIC MUTATED ANT, OUR HEROES' PLAN TO FOCUS THE SUN'S RAYS ON TO IT WITH A GIANT MAGNIFYING GLASS IS THWARTED BY A SUDDEN CHANGE IN THE WEATHER...

DON'T PANIC, AGENTS - ALL WE HAVE TO DO IS WAIT FOR THE CLOUDS TO CLEAR, AND THEN TRY AGAIN.

GRAAAAAAA!

SMASH!

OK, NOW IT MIGHT BE TIME FOR PLAN B ...

WHAT'S PLAN B?

RUN!

OOH - THAT'S A LOT BETTER THAN PLAN A!

WHY, THE LUMBERING BRUTE CAN'T KEEP UP WITH US!

BEESLEY'S RIGHT - IF WE CAN JUST KEEP RUNNING WE'LL BE SAFE!

HA! HE'LL NEVER CATCH US NOW!

JUST KEEP RUNNING!

I THINK I MIGHT HAVE DETECTED AN ERROR IN YOUR PLAN, SIR...

SKDD!

I DON'T SUPPOSE THERE'S A PLAN 'C'?

I SAY, THIS IS A BIT OF A POOR SHOW ...

OH DEAR.

I CALCULATE THAT WE ARE IN BIG TROUBLE.

SO, SUPER ANIMAL ADVENTURE SQUAD, YOU MAY HAVE FOILED MY SCHEME TO TAKE OVER TEATIME, BUT IT IS I, DOCTOR NEFARIOUS WHO SHALL HAVE THE LAST LAUGH!

HA HA HA HA HA!

TWITCH

YOU FIEND! SO THIS WAS YOUR REAL PLAN ALL ALONG; TO DOPE YOUR CAKES WITH ANT MUTAGEN X-13 AND TURN THESE PEACEFUL CREATURES INTO AN ARMY OF MUTANTS!

SCRATCH

WELL...

...ACTUALLY I JUST PUT IT IN BECAUSE IT TASTES LIKE BROCCOLI, BUT THAT'S A GOOD PLAN, TOO.

NOW, ON WITH YOUR DESTRUCTION!

HA HA HA HA HA!

ANT MUTAGEN X-13

ECONOMY SIZE

MMM TASTY!

SEE THE NEXT PAGE

SUPER ANIMAL ADVENTURE SQUAD

BY JAMES TURNER

IN: **THE TEATIME OF DOOM** PART ELEVEN

TRAPPED IN THE GRIP OF DOCTOR NEFARIOUS' GIANT ANT, OUR HEROES FACE CERTAIN DOOM... CAN ANYTHING SAVE THEM NOW?

YES, DESTROY THEM, MY MUTANT MARVEL!

DESTROY THE SUPER ANIMAL ADVENTURE SQUAD! HAHAHAHA HA!

?

WELL? WHAT ARE YOU WAITING FOR?

GET ON WITH IT!

SCRITCH SCRATCH

WHY ARE YOU LOOKING AT ME LIKE THAT...?

WINK!

WAVE!

ANT-O-VISION

TOSS!

W-WHAT ARE YOU DOING??

AKH!

HUG!

UNHAND ME, YOU IMBECILE!

WELL, I SUPPOSE THIS MEANS OUR GIANT ANT PROBLEM IS SOLVED...

SMOOCH!

AGENT K! COME IN! WHAT'S THE STATUS OF THE MISSION?

SALUTE!

THE MISSION WAS, ER, A COMPLETE SUCCESS, SIR. THE STOLEN CAKES HAVE BEEN LOCATED AND SECURED!

EXCELLENT WORK, AGENT! I'LL SEND A TEAM OF CAKE REDISTRIBUTION ENGINEERS TO TAKE THEM BACK TO THE SHOPS. TEATIME IS SAVED!

DUST DUST

DID THE SQUAD RUN INTO ANY PROBLEMS?

NOT AT ALL...

...IT WAS A PIECE OF <u>CAKE</u>!

HA HA HA HA! HA HA HA HA HO HO HO HO

GROAN

EXIT

HA HA HA HA HO HA HA HO HO HO HO HA HA HA HA HA

HELLO?

ARE WE STILL PLAYING?

ANYONE?

FREE ANT FOOD

THE END!

IT'S NOT REALLY THE END! TURN THE PAGE FOR ANOTHER THRILLING SUPER ANIMAL ADVENTURE SQUAD MISSION!

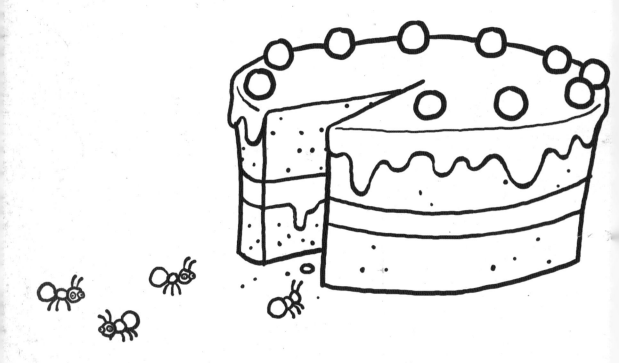

the Case of the
BABOON BANDIT

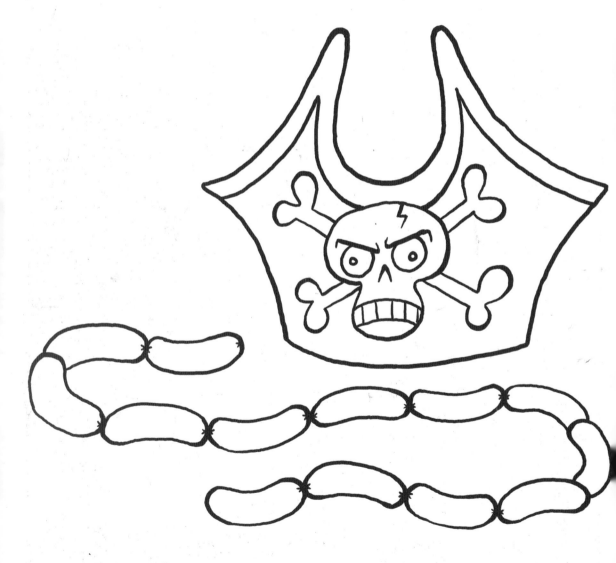

GLAAAA!

BLAPP!

DON'T WORRY, YOU CAN HAVE IT BACK ONCE MY SHOW'S FINISHED!

CHAMELEON SPIT. YUK.

NO, UH, THAT'S OK — I DON'T REALLY WANT IT ANYMORE...

OH! HE'S ABOUT TO REVEAL THE IDENTITY OF THE KILLER!

AGENT K

CHEW!

EDGE OF THE SEAT!

AND SO I CAN REVEAL ZAT ZEE CULPRIT IS NONE OTHER THAN...

AGENT K!

GASP! AGENT K WAS THE KILLER!? I NEVER SAW THAT COMING!

AGENT K COME IN!

THERE'S BEEN A BURGLARY!

AGENT K REPORTING, SIR! BUT IF YOU DON'T MIND MY SAYING, ISN'T A BURGLARY A MATTER FOR THE POLICE, NOT AN ELITE TEAM OF ANTHROPOMORPHIC SECRET AGENTS?

BUT THIS WAS NO ORDINARY BURGLARY, AGENT... THIS WAS A BABOON BURGLARY!

PRANCING PRIMATES! YOU DON'T MEAN...

I'M AFRAID SO, AGENT: SOMEONE HAS STOLEN THE WORLD'S MOST BEAUTIFUL AND PRICELESS ARTEFACT...

...THE LEGENDARY JADE BABOON OF RANGOON!

THE FIENDS!

DIAMONDS

RUBIES

THE BABOON MUST BE RECOVERED! I WANT YOUR TEAM TO GO TO THE MUSEUM OF INCALCULABLY PRICELESS TREASURES AND GET TO THE BOTTOM OF THIS AT ONCE.

DON'T WORRY, SIR — MY TEAM WILL GET TO THE BOTTOM OF THIS BABOON IN NO TIME!

GOOD LUCK, AGENT! OVER AND OUT!

ALRIGHT, AGENTS, IT'S TIME FOR ACTION!

BUT IT'S ALMOST TEATIME.

YOU SAID WE COULD HAVE SPONGE FINGERS!

ELEMENTARY, MY DEAR HASTINGS!

THE DELICIOUS BISCUITY TREATS WILL HAVE TO WAIT, AGENTS: WE'VE GOT A VILLAIN TO CATCH!

CAN WE BRING MINI ROLLS?

OK, BUT ONLY ONE EACH.

AW.

AGENT BEARBOT, AGENT BEESLEY, ARE YOU READY TO GO?

MY READINESS SUBROUTINES ARE ACTIVATED, SIR!

AGENT BEESLEY

AGENT BEARBOT

WEIR.

WE'LL SHOW THOSE CADS WHAT FOR!

THEN THERE'S NO TIME TO LOSE... TO THE MUSEUM!

OOH! CAN WE GO TO THE GIFT SHOP?

WHO CAN BE BEHIND THIS DESPICABLE CRIME?

SUPER ANIMAL ADVENTURE SQUAD

BY JAMES TURNER — PART TWO

THE CASE OF THE BABOON BANDIT

THE WORLD'S MOST VALUABLE TREASURE, THE LEGENDARY JADE BABOON OF RANGOON, HAS BEEN STOLEN, AND IT'S UP TO THE SQUAD TO FIND THE VILLAIN BEHIND THE THEFT...

OH DEAR, OH DEAR, OH DEAR ...

WHEREVER CAN THEY BE?

GRACIOUS ME! NOT ANOTHER BREAK-IN!?

CRASH!

OH MY!

DAVIDANGELO'S STATUE OF MICHAEL!

... BUT I HARDLY TOUCHED IT ...

REMEMBER WHAT WE TALKED ABOUT, REX: ANCIENT RELICS ARE NOT POSEABLE ACTION FIGURES.

AH, YOU MUST BE THE MUSEUM CURATOR! WELL YOU HAVE NOTHING TO FEAR NOW — THE SUPER ANIMAL ADVENTURE SQUAD IS HERE TO SAVE THE DAY!

DON'T WORRY, REX, WE CAN FIX IT. NOW, WHERE'S THE OTHER HAND?

OH, I CAN SEE A SPARE ONE OVER THERE.

GLUE

WHAT WAS THAT??

CRASH!

NOTHING YOU NEED TO WORRY ABOUT — NOW CAN YOU SHOW US WHERE THE CRIME TOOK PLACE?

AND SO... THIS IS WHERE WE KEPT THE LEGENDARY JADE BABOON OF RANGOON. I JUST CAN'T IMAGINE WHO COULD HAVE DONE SUCH A TERRIBLE THING!

VILLAINY CAN TAKE MANY FORMS, CURATOR. THAT'S ONE OF THE THINGS THAT MAKES IT SO VILLAINOUS.

THIS SIDE ON FACE

STAND BACK! WITH MY SUPERIOR DETECTING SKILLS I'LL HAVE THIS CASE SOLVED IN NO TIME!

OH MY!

MOANY LISA

HMM... THIS SANDWICH IS DEFINITELY A CLUE!

UM, ACTUALLY, I THINK THAT'S MY DINNER...

I DETECT... EGG MAYONNAISE!

OK, I WANT THE REST OF YOU TO SPLIT INTO TWO TEAMS: BEARBOT, BEESLEY, YOU'LL HELP ME TO LOOK FOR CLUES, REX, YOU'RE IN CHARGE OF TRYING NOT TO BREAK ANYTHING.

YES, SIR!

HMM... THESE TRACKS ARE QUITE FASCINATING!

I DEDUCE THAT THE SCOUNDREL HAD A WOODEN LEG!

MY SENSORS INDICATE THAT THESE FEATHERS COME FROM A BIRD OF THE PSITTACIDAE FAMILY.

I CALCULATE THAT THE THIEF MUST OWN A PARROT!

OH! OH! AND I FOUND A TAIL!

I BET IT'S FROM SOME SORT OF GROSS LIZARD!

THAT'S YOUR TAIL, REX.

OH. RIGHT.

...AND THESE ORANGE PEELS CAN ONLY MEAN OUR CULPRIT WAS TRYING TO STAVE OFF THE EFFECTS OF SCURVY.

CLEARLY WE'RE LOOKING FOR SOMEONE WHO SPENDS A LOT OF TIME AT SEA!

LET'S SEE NOW... A WOODEN LEG... OWNS A PARROT... SPENDS A LOT OF TIME AT SEA...

WHY, EVEN A BUFFOON SHOULD BE ABLE TO IDENTIFY THE PERPETRATOR FROM THIS EVIDENCE!

OH! OH! LET ME TRY! LET ME TRY!

AHOY, REX, YE CAN DO IT!

HMM...

IT WAS A CLOWN! QUICKLY! I'LL GET THE DISGUISES!

ARRR...

SLAP!

I STAND CORRECTED.

IF I MIGHT INTERRUPT, I COMPUTE THAT THERE IS A 98.7% PROBABILITY THAT THE BABOON WAS STOLEN BY NONE OTHER THAN THE DREAD PIRATE GREEN BEARD HIMSELF!

REMARKABLE! YOU COULD TELL THAT FROM JUST THOSE FEW CLUES?

GREEN BEARD TOTALLY RULES

Sincerely, Green Beard

WELL, THE SIGN ON THE WALL WAS A BIT OF A HINT, TOO.

THAT SETTLES IT: IT LOOKS LIKE WE'RE TAKING A TRIP... TO PIRATE'S COVE!

IS THAT WHERE THE CLOWNS LIVE?

WHAT AWAITS AT PIRATE'S COVE?

★ SUPER ANIMAL ADVENTURE SQUAD ★

BY JAMES TURNER

PART THREE

THE CASE OF THE BABOON BANDIT

THE WORLD'S MOST PRICELESS TREASURE, THE JADE BABOON OF RANGOON, HAS BEEN STOLEN, AND THE SQUAD HAS DISCOVERED THAT THE CULPRIT IS NONE OTHER THAN THE DREAD PIRATE GREEN BEARD!

WELL, AGENTS, HERE WE ARE: PIRATE'S COVE!

AND THERE'S GREEN BEARD'S SHIP: 'THE SAUCY PIGLET'!

...BUT IT'S GUARDED BY HIS BEST MEN...

SAY, WHAT'S THE 18TH LETTER OF THE ALPHABET?

ARRRR!

OH, SO IT IS!

I HAVE A PLAN, SIR: I'LL GO ABOARD, FIND GREEN BEARD, AND ASK HIM NICELY TO GIVE THE BABOON BACK!

DO YOU REALLY THINK THAT WILL WORK...?

DON'T WORRY, SIR, I'M FULLY PREPARED TO SAY 'PRETTY PLEASE' IF NECESSARY!

I SAY! HELLO THERE! WOULD YOU KIND GENTLEMEN MIND LETTING ME ABOARD SO I CAN HAVE A LITTLE CHAT WITH YOUR CAPTAIN?

I THINK THE REST OF US HAD BETTER LAY LOW UNTIL WE SEE HOW AGENT BEARBOT GETS ON...

GOSH, YOU REALLY ARE A FRIENDLY BUNCH!

10 MINUTES LATER...

HOW'S THE DIPLOMATIC MISSION PROCEEDING, AGENT?

FISH

OH, IT'S GOING QUITE SPLENDIDLY, SIR. THE PIRATES HAVE WELCOMED ME AS ONE OF THEIR OWN.

IN FACT THEY'VE EVEN ASKED ME TO JOIN IN WITH ONE OF THEIR TRADITIONAL GAMES...

I'M NOT QUITE SURE WHAT THE RULES ARE, THOUGH...

IT LOOKS LIKE IT MIGHT BE TIME FOR PLAN B...

GO HOME FOR TEA?

SPLASH!

DYNAMITE?

NOT QUITE...

THE PLAN IS THIS: WE WALK IN THERE AND TAKE BACK THE BABOON FROM RIGHT UNDER THEIR NOSES...

...IN DISGUISE!

OH BOY! DRESS UP!

AGENT IRWIN: OPEN UP!

NOW, LET'S SEE WHAT WE HAVE IN HERE...

GLAKK!

RUMMAGE!

AN EYEPATCH...

...A CUTLASS...

GLK! SO THAT'S WHERE MY CUTLASS WENT!

EW! MOIST!

...A FALSE BEARD...
...A STUFFED PARROT...

...HMM...

WHAT'S THIS?

THAT'TH MY TONGUE, THIR.

I SEE... WELL TRY NOT TO GET IT MIXED UP WITH THE DISGUISES IN FUTURE.

SOME TIME LATER...

RIGHT, AGENTS, IT'S TIME TO INSPECT YOUR COSTUMES!

AH - GOOD WORK, AGENT BEARBOT!...

THANK YOU, SIR!

FLIP

FLAP

EXCELLENT JOB, AGENT BEESLEY...

THOSE BLIGHTERS WON'T KNOW WHAT HIT THEM, EH?

REX, WE'RE SUPPOSED TO BE DRESSING AS PIRATES. PLEASE TRY AGAIN.

OHHH, PIRATES...

WHY DO I HAVE TO BE THE PARROT?

BECAUSE YOU'RE THE ONLY ONE WITH WINGS AND A BEAK, IRWIN.

THAT'S DISCRIMINATION!

WELL, I DO HAVE THIS BARNACLE COSTUME IF YOU'D PREFER...?

SIGH... PIECES OF EIGHT! PIECES OF EIGHT! CAW!

BILLY BARNACLE

AHOY CAPTAIN!

I THINK WE NEED TO HAVE A LITTLE TALK, REX...

WILL THE SQUAD'S CUNNING DISGUISES FOOL THE PIRATES?

SUPER ANIMAL ADVENTURE SQUAD

BY JAMES TURNER

PART FOUR

THE CASE OF THE BABOON BANDIT

PIRATES HAVE STOLEN THE WORLD'S MOST VALUABLE TREASURE, THE JADE BABOON OF RANGOON, AND NOW THE SQUAD (WEARING CUNNING DISGUISES) MUST SNEAK ABOARD THE SHIP AND TRY TO GET IT BACK...

ABOARD THE DREAD PIRATE GREEN BEARD'S SHIP, 'THE SAUCY PIGLET', THE CREW ARE UP TO THEIR USUAL VILLAINOUS DEEDS...

FOUR DOWN, WHAT'S THE MISSING WORD: "I AM, HE IS, YOU___"

ARRRRR!

OH, YES, WELL DONE!

WRITE WRITE

LET'S SEE... FIVE ACROSS: A COMMON ABBREVIATION FOR THE WORD 'RADIUS'.

AHOY THERE!

DON'T MIND US, WE'RE JUST A BAND OF COMPLETELY ORDINARY PIRATES, GOING ABOUT OUR COMPLETELY ORDINARY PIRATEY BUSINESS! NO NEED TO PAY US ANY ATTENTION.

HULLO!

ARE YOU SURE YOU'RE PIRATES?

OH, YES, QUITE SURE. BEEN PIRATES ALL OUR LIVES, ISN'T THAT RIGHT, MEN?

OH, I SHOULD JOLLY WELL SAY SO! PIRATES TO THE CORE, WHOT?

GLOWER

YEE-HAW! GIDDY-UP!

INTERNAL DIAGNOSTICS INDICATE THAT I HAVE BEEN A PIRATE FOR 17.38 YEARS

UM...POLLY WANT A CRACKER...?

WELL, IF YOU'LL EXCUSE US WE'RE VERY BUSY... DECKS TO SWAB, MAINBRACES TO SPLICE...

NOT SO FAST!

ULP!

...YOUR PARROT'S FALLEN OFF YOUR SHOULDER!

WHO? ME?

I'LL GIVE YOU A HAND!

OOF, YOU MIGHT WANT TO LAY OFF THE CRACKERS THERE, POLLY!

HEY! YOU CAN TALK! UH...I MEAN, PRETTY POLLY!

URGG... UM... THANKS...

NO PROBLEM! HAVE A NICE DAY!

OK, AGENTS, IT LOOKS LIKE WE'VE FOOLED THEM. I WANT YOU TO FAN OUT AND FIND OUT WHERE THEY'RE KEEPING THE BABOON.

AND WHATEVER YOU DO, MAKE SURE YOU DON'T DRAW ANY ATTENTION TO YOURSELVES!

OOF!

THUD!!

SO...

HELLOOO! ANY BABOONS IN THERE?

HMM...NOT UNDER HERE...

HAND OVER THE BABOON, YOU CUR, OR I SHALL BE FORCED TO RUN YOU THROUGH!

ZZZ

I'D BETTER CHECK TO SEE IF IT'S AT THE BOTTOM OF THIS BARREL...

GLUCK GLUCK

SORRY, SIR, WE'VE SEARCHED EVERY INCH OF THIS SHIP—THE BABOON IS NOWHERE TO BE FOUND.

THE FIENDS ARE CLEVERER THAN I THOUGHT!

THEY'VE OBVIOUSLY HIDDEN IT IN A PLACE SO CUNNING THAT IT'S ALMOST IMPOSSIBLE TO DETECT!

OH! MAYBE IT'S IN THERE?

TREASURE ROOM

WELL, I SUPPOSE IT'S WORTH A TRY...

BLISTERING BUCCANEERS!

THERE IT IS...

...THE JADE BABOON OF RANGOON!

WILL OUR HEROES BE ABLE TO ESCAPE THE SHIP WITH THE PRICELESS PRIMATE?

SUPER ANIMAL ADVENTURE SQUAD

BY JAMES TURNER

PART FIVE

THE CASE OF THE BABOON BANDIT

GREEN BEARD THE PIRATE HAS STOLEN THE WORLD'S MOST PRICELESS ARTEFACT, THE LEGENDARY JADE BABOON OF RANGOON, AND OUR HEROES HAVE SNUCK ABOARD HIS SHIP IN ORDER TO GET IT BACK...

ALRIGHT, SQUAD. AGENT BEESLEY AND I WILL GO IN AND GRAB THE BABOON, THE REST OF YOU KEEP WATCH OUT HERE AND LET US KNOW IF ANYONE COMES.

THIS SHIP IS FULL OF PIRATES, SO WE NEED TO FIND A WAY TO GET THE BABOON OUT WITHOUT A SOUND...

UNDERSTOOD, OLD BEAN, AND I HAVE JUST THE THING FOR THE TASK!

SSSSSSS

ACTUALLY, BEESLEY, I WAS THINKING WE MIGHT PICK THE LOCK.

SST!

PICK THE LOCK, EH? A LITTLE UNDERHAND, BUT NEEDS MUST AND ALL THAT, I SUPPOSE.

IT SHOULD BE EASY ENOUGH, I JUST NEED SOMETHING SMALL AND SHARP TO PUT IN THE KEY HOLE...

SMALL AND SHARP, EH?

WELL I'M SURE I'LL BE ABLE TO RUSTLE UP SOMETHING THAT—

GRAB!

I SAY!

I KNEW YOU'D BE THE PERFECT AGENT FOR THIS JOB, BEESLEY.

THIS IS MOST UNDIGNIFIED!

CLICK!

DONE IT! NOW LET'S GRAB THE BABOON AND GET OUT OF HERE!

THAT MIGHT BE EASIER SAID THAN DONE...

WHY'S THAT?

GRRR!

OH.

GRRR!

IT LOOKS LIKE A BIT OF A STICKY SITUATION, OLD CHUM.

COOKERY WIZARDS? MAGIC SPOONS? YOU LOT ARE A COUPLE OF DUBLOONS SHORT OF A TREASURE CHEST.

THIS IS ALL TOO SILLY - I'M GOING HOME TO WATCH NEIGHBOURS!

SO - YE DARE TO QUESTION THE POWER OF THE BABOON MOON SPOON OF RANGOON?

YES, I DOON.

ALA-KA...

...CUMBERLAND!

OH!

SAUSAGE SWOOSH!

URK!

SO, WHAT DO YE THINK O' THE POWER O' THE SPOON NOW?

DELICIOUS!

CHOM!

BUT WHAT DO YOU, THE WORLD'S MOST FEARSOME PIRATE, WANT WITH A MAGIC SPOON?

ER, WELL...

COUGH

ARR! CREWMAN, LEAVE US ALONE FOR A FEW MINUTES - I CAN HANDLE THESE SCURVY SWABS ON ME OWN!

AYE SIR!

YE SEE, THE THING IS...

I HATE BEING A PIRATE!

YOU - YOU DO?

AYE! EVER SINCE I WAS JUST A LAD THERE WAS ONLY ONE THING I EVER WANTED TO BE...

A-AND WHAT WAS THAT...?

A TV CHEF!

WILL GREEN BEARD'S CULINARY DREAMS COME TRUE?

SUPER ANIMAL ADVENTURE SQUAD

BY JAMES TURNER — PART SEVEN

THE CASE OF THE BABOON BANDIT

HAVING STOLEN A MAGIC SPOON AND CAPTURED THE SUPER ANIMAL ADVENTURE SQUAD, THE DREAD PIRATE GREEN BEARD HAS JUST REVEALED A SURPRISING SECRET...

YOU WANT TO BE A... TV CHEF??

AYE! BUT ME FATHER WOULD NEVER ALLOW IT.

ARRR! I TRY TO RAISE YE TO BE A GOOD PIRATE AND THIS IS HOW YE REPAY ME?

WITH COOKERY??

STIR

GREEN BEARD AGED 12 YRS

HONESTLY, I DON'T KNOW WHAT TO DO WITH THAT BOY SOMETIMES...

WAAAAA!

I'M SURE IT'S JUST A PHASE, DEAR.

OH BOO HOO HOO HOO!

THERE, THERE ...

PAT PAT

WHY DON'T YOU JUST GIVE US BACK THE BABOON AND THE SPOON AND WE'LL GET YOU SOME NICE COOKERY CLASSES...

NEVER! I'LL BE NEEDING ALL O' THE SPOON'S POWER TO COMPLETE ME PLAN...

WIPE

ME PLAN TO BE CROWNED AS THE WORLD'S GREATEST CHEF!

BATTLE OF THE SPATULAS
CHEF OF THE YEAR

WHEN: TOMORROW!
WHERE: ON BOARD THE SAUCY PIGLET
PRIZE: YOU GET TO TELL EVERYONE THAT YOU ARE TOTALLY CHEF OF THE YEAR

OOH, YOU CAN'T USE A MAGIC SPOON TO WIN A COOKERY COMPETITION ...THAT'S CHEATING!

HM, THAT'S A GOOD POINT, BUT YE BE FORGETTING ONE THING...

I DON'T CARE!

YAA!

THPT!

OH, I SEE.

HA, YOU SIMPLETON! YOU MAY HAVE A MAGIC SPOON, BUT YOU WILL BE COMPETING AGAINST THE FINEST CHEFS IN THE WORLD.

YOU SHALL NEVER TRIUMPH OVER THEM, NOT WHILE YOUR EVERY DISH IS TAINTED WITH THE BITTER TASTE OF DECEIT!

AYE, IT'S TRUE. THE OTHER CHEFS MIGHT BEAT ME, BUT I DON'T THINK WE NEED TO WORRY ABOUT THEM...

AND WHY IS THAT, PRAY TELL?

GADZOOKS!

BECAUSE I HAVE THEM ALL LOCKED UP HERE IN MY CUPBOARD! HA HA!

HELP!

I HAD TO EAT MY HAT.

STOP POKING ME WITH YOUR LADLE!

NOW NOTHING CAN STOP ME WINNING, AND THAT'S JUST THE BEGINNING OF ME EVIL PLAN...

..I'LL HAVE ME OWN TV SHOW...

...ME OWN SERIES OF COOK BOOKS...

...ME OWN BRAND OF GREEN BEARD'S FISH FINGERS!

I'LL RULE THE WORLD!

(OF COOKERY)

BOOM

CRACK!

WU HA HA!

HA HA HA!

...HA HA HA HA HA HA HA HA HA HA HA HA HA!

AHEM...

EXCUSE ME...?

TAP TAP

WHAT IS IT?

YES?

UM, IT'S ABOUT YOUR EVIL PLAN...

WELL, I DON'T MEAN TO BE RUDE, BUT... WELL, IT'S NOT VERY...EVIL IS IT?

I-IT'S NOT?

NO, WELL NOT ENOUGH TO QUALIFY FOR ALL THE LIGHTNING AND SINISTER LAUGHTER.

AW! BUT I PAID EXTRA FOR THE LIGHTNING!

DANGLE!

CAUTION: BLAH BLAH RADIATION LEVELS

WELL, NOT TO WORRY, I'M SURE IF YOU ADD A LITTLE SOMETHING YOU CAN MAKE IT MUCH MORE EVIL.

HMM... I COULD MAKE YOU ALL WEAR REALLY THICK SWEATERS AND THEN REFUSE TO OPEN THE WINDOW?

THAT'S GOOD, BUT MAYBE YOU COULD GO A TEENY BIT MORE EVIL,

OH... I COULD... I COULD... I COULD MAKE YOU ALL WALK THE PLANK!

OH YES, THAT'S PERFECT! WELL DONE!

SHAKE!

I COULDN'T HAVE DONE IT WITHOUT YE!

SO...

WU HA HA HA HA!

NICE WORK, AGENT BEARBOT.

I'M ALWAYS HAPPY TO HELP, SIR!

OH NO! I FORGOT TO BRING MY TRUNKS!

WILL OUR HEROES BE GOING FOR A DIP?

ALRIGHT, YE SCURVY SWABS, IT LOOKS LIKE YE DO GET A LAST REQUEST. SO, DID YE HAVE SOMETHING IN MIND?

OH, I THINK WE CAN COME UP WITH SOMETHING...

~WINK~

OOH! COULD WE HAVE SOME CAKE?

REX!

ARR! I THOUGHT YE'D NEVER ASK!

NO REX! WHAT ABOUT THE PLAN?

PLAN...?

ONE CAKE, COMING RIGHT UP!

ABRA - KA - MARZIPAN!

MAGIC!

OOH!

DIG IN!

HAPPY PLANK-WALK!

I SAY!

SHORTLY...

SO... HOW WAS IT??

SPECTRO CHEMICAL ANALYSIS INDICATES THAT IT WAS 19% TASTY, 34% SCRUMPTIOUS AND 47% CAKE-A-LICIOUS.

BURRRP!

OH! YOU'RE TOO KIND!

NOW, ON WITH THE KILLING!

AW.

WELL WE'RE ABOUT TO BE FED TO THE SHARKS, REX. I HOPE YOU FEEL BAD ABOUT ASKING FOR 'CAKE'.

HEY, NOT IN THE STOMACH!

I DO.

PROD

... I SHOULD HAVE SAID CHOCOLATE CAKE!

JAB!

WELL THAT'S THE END OF THE SUPER ANIMAL ADVENTURE SQUAD - NOW NOTHING CAN STOP ME! NOTHING!

IS THE SQUAD REALLY SHARK FOOD?

36

ARR! NOW THAT THE

SUPER ANIMAL ADVENTURE SQUAD

ARE SLEEPING AT THE BOTTOM O' THE OCEAN, NOTHING CAN STOP ME WINNIN' THE BATTLE O' THE SPATULAS COOKERY COMPETITION!

THE CASE OF THE BABOON BANDIT

PART NINE

BY JAMES TURNER

BUT...

CRE-E-EAK

EW! 'ITH 'ANK ITH AN 'AWTY!*

BY JOVE! WE'RE SAVED!

EXCELLENT WORK, AGENT REX!

DEFINE 'SAVED'...

YOU KNOW, SIR, YOUR HEELS AREN'T DRY AT ALL...

* EW! THIS PLANK IS ALL SALTY!

WHY, WHAT AN EXCELLENT CHANCE TO STUDY THE LOCAL SEA-LIFE...

GOODNESS, WHAT FRIENDLY FISH!

BITE!

CHOMP!

LEAP!

JUMP!

CR-A-CK

BEND

I SAY, IT SEEMS THE ADDED WEIGHT OF BEAR-BOT'S AQUATIC CHUMS IS PUTTING A BIT OF STRAIN ON THE OLD PLANK.

I KNEW I SHOULD HAVE STAYED IN BED THIS MORNING.

PERMISSION TO DISEMBARK AND REJOIN THE SQUAD LATER, SIR?

GRANTED.

GOOD LUCK, SIR!

DROP!

SPLOOSH!

SPRO1-O1-OING!

AAAAAH!

SAY!

AAAAH!

AAAAH!

AAAH!

AAAH!

AAAH!

WELL THIS IS A BIT OF A RUM DO, WOT?

OOF!

THUD! WHUMP!

PULSATING PARABOLAS! WE'VE LANDED BACK ON THE DECK OF THE SAUCY PIGLET! WE'RE SAFE!

SAFE APART FROM ALL THE PIRATES WHO JUST TRIED TO KILL US, YOU MEAN?

OH, YES.

SO IT LOOKS LIKE THE PLANK WILL BE GETTING A SECOND USE TODAY...

UM, ACTUALLY SIR, RULE 32 SAYS NO ONE IS ALLOWED TO WALK THE PLANK TWICE IN ONE DAY...

BLAST THIS CURSED BUREAUCRACY!

WELL THEN, LET'S KEELHAUL THE SWABS INSTEAD!

I'M AFRAID WE JUST PAINTED THE HULL YESTERDAY.

IT'S STILL TACKY.

CAN WE HANG THEM FROM THE YARD-ARM?

IT'S GOT LAUNDRY ON IT.

CAN WE AT LEAST GIVE THEM A TASTE O' THE CAT O' NINE TAILS??

IT'S AT THE VET.

ARRR!

ALRIGHT! ALRIGHT! JUST THROW 'EM IN THE BRIG AND I'LL DEAL WITH 'EM AFTER THE COMPETITION!

AYE SIR!

SO... I'VE GOT TO GET OUT OF HERE! I'M MISSING DOCTOR WHO!

I JUST WISH THE PRISONERS IN THE NEXT CELL WOULD STOP SINGING ABOUT COOKING...

YOU PUT THE BUTTER IN, AND YOU STIR IT AROUND, AND THAT'S WHAT IT'S ALL ABOUT... OOOH CAKEY CAKEY CAKEY! OOOH BAKEY BAKEY BAKEY!...

COOKING?...IT'S THE WORLD'S GREATEST CHEFS! BUT I THOUGHT YOU WERE LOCKED IN THE CAPTAIN'S CABIN?

YES, BUT HE THREW US DOWN HERE AFTER WE SANG 42 VERSES OF '99 BOTTLES OF SPICE IN THE RACK'...

WELL WITH ALL OF YOU LOCKED UP HERE I SUPPOSE THERE'S NOTHING TO STOP GREEN BEARD USING THE MOON SPOON OF RANGOON TO WIN THE BATTLE OF THE SPATULAS...

GASP!

DID YOU SAY THAT GREEN BEARD HAS THE MOON SPOON?

YES, I...

IF WHAT YOU SAY IS TRUE THEN THERE IS MORE THAN A COOKERY COMPETITION AT STAKE...

THE FATE OF THE ENTIRE WORLD IS IN THE BALANCE!

NEXT PAGE: THE CURSE OF THE MOON SPOON!

SUPER ANIMAL ADVENTURE SQUAD

BY JAMES TURNER — PART TEN

THE CASE OF THE BABOON BANDIT

OUR HEROES HAVE BEEN IMPRISONED IN THE BRIG OF THE PIRATE SHIP, 'THE SAUCY PIGLET', WHERE THEY HAVE MET A MYSTERIOUS STRANGER WITH A TERRIFYING TALE TO TELL...

WHO—WHO ARE YOU?

I AM EMESS-JI, KING OF THE CHEFS!

REGAL!

I KNOW ALL THE SECRETS OF CHEF-KIND: THE MOON SPOON OF RANGOON, THE SIEVE OF SOLOMON, THE OVEN GLOVE OF ENSORSCELMENT — ALL ARE KNOWN TO ME!

I ALSO KNOW AN EXCELLENT RECIPE FOR SPOTTED DICK.

KISS

BUT, YOUR MAJESTY, I DON'T UNDERSTAND HOW THE MOON SPOON CAN ENDANGER THE WORLD?

THAT IS BECAUSE YOU DO NOT KNOW OF THE CURSE LAID UPON IT BY GORD-ONRAM-SEY AS HE WAS BEING LED AWAY TO JAIL...

1000 YEARS EARLIER... I LAY THIS CURSE UPON YOU: WHEN BEARD OF EMERALD WIELDS SPOON OF MOON THE END OF THE BATTLE SHALL SEAL YOUR DOOM

FOR IF BEARD AND SPOON SHOULD WIN THAT DAY THE WORLD SHALL BE TURNED...
... TO LEMON SOUFFLÉ!

... LEMON SOUFFLÉ?

WELL IT WAS THE ONLY THING I COULD THINK OF THAT RHYMED WITH 'DAY'!

SORRY.

PANDEMONIOUS PROPHECIES! BEARD OF EMERALD? BATTLE? DO YOU KNOW WHAT THIS MEANS?

THAT CHEFS SHOULD NEVER BE ALLOWED TO WRITE POETRY?

IF WE CAN'T STOP GREEN BEARD FROM WINNING THE COMPETITION, THE ENTIRE WORLD WILL TURN INTO A LEMON SOUFFLÉ!

GASP!

GREAT SCOTT!

YAY!

WHAT?

I LIKE LEMON SOUFFLÉ...

WE HAVE TO GET OUT OF HERE AND STOP GREEN BEARD FROM WINNING THE BATTLE OF THE SPATULAS!

LUCKILY I'M SURE THAT AGENT BEARBOT IS ALREADY WORKING ON A DARING RESCUE PLAN...

MEANWHILE, AT THE BOTTOM OF THE OCEAN...

EXCUSE ME, I DON'T SUPPOSE YOU'VE SEEN A PIRATE SHIP ANYWHERE AROUND HERE, HAVE YOU?

I CAN BEAR THIS INFERNAL INCARCERATION NO LONGER!

WOULD THAT THESE VILE BARS DID NOT CONSTRAIN ME!

★ SUPER ANIMAL ADVENTURE SQUAD ★

BY JAMES TURNER

PART ELEVEN

THE CASE OF THE BABOON BANDIT

THE SQUAD HAS CHALLENGED THE DREAD PIRATE GREEN BEARD TO A COOKERY COMPETITION – BUT IF THEY LOSE THE ENTIRE WORLD WILL TURN INTO A LEMON SOUFFLÉ!

WAIT, I KNOW A RECIPE – MY AUNT DORIS' NEVER-FAIL CHOCOLATE BROWNIES! NOTHING TASTES NICER THAN THEM!

THEN MAYBE WE STILL HAVE A CHANCE... TO THE GALLEY!

IN THE GALLEY...

RIGHT REX, THE FATE OF THE WORLD RESTS ON YOUR BROWNIES – GET COOKING!

OK – BRING ME TWO PINTS OF VINEGAR AND A BAG OF ONIONS!

YES SIR!

SALUTE!

UM – ARE YOU SURE YOU REMEMBER YOUR AUNT'S RECIPE, REX...?

DON'T WORRY, SIR, EVERYTHING IS UNDER CONTROL

5 MINUTES LATER...

AAAH!

COUGH! IRWIN! QUICK, OPEN THE WINDOW!

ARE YOU SURE...

DO IT!

AKH! CLOSE IT! CLOSE IT!

SPLOOSH!

I WISH YOU'D MAKE YOUR MIND UP.

WELL, AT LEAST THE FIRE'S OUT...

TIC TIC

RRRRIIIIINNNGGGG

IT'S READY! WHO WANTS A TASTE?

I'LL GIVE IT A TRY...

REX! YOU SAID YOU KNEW THE RECIPE FOR YOUR AUNT DORIS' BROWNIES!

RALP!

WELL NOW I COME TO THINK ABOUT IT, I'M NOT ACTUALLY SURE I HAVE AN AUNT DORIS...

ALRIGHT, THE WORLD IS DOOMED UNLESS WE CAN WIN THIS COOKERY COMPETITION AND ALL WE HAVE IS A SOGGY, BURNED, FISH-COVERED MESS THAT IRWIN HAS BEEN SICK ON...

GROOO

BUT LET'S NOT PANIC — PERHAPS WE STILL HAVE TIME TO MAKE AN OMELETTE OR SOMETHING...

TIME'S UP! BRING YOUR DISH UPSTAIRS FOR JUDGING!

OK, NOW WE CAN PANIC.

MMM-FISHY!

41

★ SUPER ★ ANIMAL ADVENTURE SQUAD

BY JAMES TURNER

PART TWELVE

THE CASE OF THE BABOON BANDIT

OUR HEROES HAVE BEATEN GREEN BEARD THE PIRATE IN A COOKERY COMPETITION TO WIN BACK THE WORLD'S MOST VALUABLE TREASURE, BUT CAN THEY ESCAPE THE PIRATE'S SHIP ALIVE?...

WELL IT LOOKS LIKE YOU OWE US ONE JADE BABOON, GREEN BEARD!

BAH! TAKE IT, FOR ALL THE GOOD IT'S DONE ME! SOB!

VICTORY!

AND THIS SCURVY SPOON WAS NO USE TO ME EITHER!

CRACK!

AVARST!

PFOOF!

ARRR...

ME LIFE IS A PATCHWORK O' REGRETS.

TRANSMOGRI-PIED!

WE DID IT! WE WON THE COMPETITION, SAVED THE WORLD, RECOVERED THE JADE BABOON, AND TURNED THE WORLD'S MOST DANGEROUS PIRATE INTO A LEMON SOUFFLÉ...

STAY BACK!

... AND IT'S NOT EVEN TEATIME YET!

DON'T WORRY, OLD BOY, I'VE TAKEN CARE OF EVERYTHING, WE'LL BE OUT OF THE CLUTCHES OF THESE NE'ER-DO-WELLS IN, OH, AROUND 8 SECONDS.

UM, WEREN'T YOU LISTENING, BEESLEY? WE ALREADY WON. WE'RE SAFE!

AH, IN THAT CASE IT SEEMS I MAY HAVE ERRED SOMEWHAT...

CAUTION GUNPOWDER STOREROOM

DANGER

SAFETY FIRST

GUN POWDER

GUN POWDER

FSSSS

AAAAH!

WEEE!

ARR, ME CRUST!

BLAST

01, KEEP THE NOISE DOWN!

KA BOOM

YOU ARE DEFINITELY GETTING A DEMERIT FOR THIS, AGENT BEESLEY.

AGENT BEARBOT, ACTIVATE AQUATIC RESCUE MODE!

YES, SIR!

AQUATIC RESCUE MODE ACTIVATED!

WELL, WE'RE ALIVE, BUT THE WORLD'S MOST VALUABLE TREASURE IS LOST FOR EVER, SOMEWHERE AT THE BOTTOM OF THE OCEAN.

COUGH

MMF MMF

SAY, WHAT HAVE YOU GOT IN YOUR MOUTH THERE, IRWIN?

MMF! ME, FIR? MUFFING! ...

SERENDIPITOUS SIMIANS! THE JADE BABOON OF RANGOON!

WELL HOW EVER DID THAT GET IN THERE?

EARLIER...

AND THE WINNER IS...

I'M SURE NO ONE WILL MISS THIS...

YOU'VE SAVED THE DAY AGAIN, IRWIN! WELL DONE!

COUGH! ER, YES, THAT'S EXACTLY WHAT I MEANT TO DO...

SLAP!

KA-CHING!

SUPER ANIMAL ADVENTURE SQUAD, COME IN! WHAT'S THE STATUS OF YOUR MISSION?

SUCCESS, SIR! THE JADE BABOON HAS BEEN RECOVERED!

YIPE!

EXCELLENT WORK, AGENTS! IN THAT CASE YOU SHOULD HAVE NO PROBLEM WITH YOUR NEXT MISSION:

THE WORLD'S GREATEST CHEFS HAVE DISAPPEARED AND IT'S UP TO YOU TO FIND OUT WHAT...

CH-CHEFS? UH ... SORRY, SIR, I DIDN'T QUITE CATCH THAT, WE, ER, MUST BE GOING INTO A TUNNEL...

KZZZKKKZZ! KKZZKZK!

HELLO? AGENT K? ARE YOU RECEIVING ME? HELL—

SIGH ... IT LOOKS LIKE IT'S GOING TO BE A LONG JOURNEY HOME. WE'D BE IN REAL TROUBLE IF WE HADN'T PACKED ALL THOSE RATIONS...

COULD YOU HAND ME THE RATION SACK, REX?

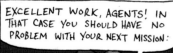

UM...

I THOUGHT IT WAS FOR THE DOLPHINS...

DOLPHINS?

YES, DOLPHINS!

MEANWHILE, SOMEWHERE IN THE MIDDLE OF THE OCEAN...

ZIS IS ZE WORST COCONUT FLAN I 'AVE EVER TASTED!

OH, SHUT UP.

SHOO!

THE END.

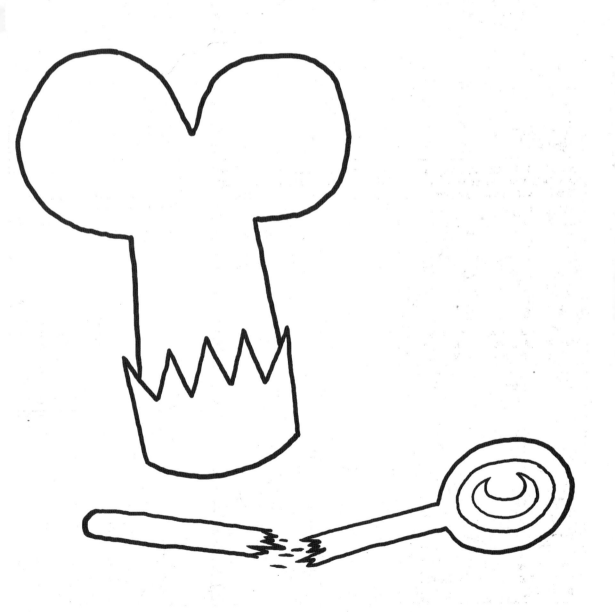

CONFIDENTIAL : AGENT PROFILES

CODENAME : AGENT K
SPECIAL SKILLS : THWARTING EVIL,
FOILING SCHEMES,
SAVING WORLD
DISLIKES : VILLAINS
LIKES : JUSTICE, LIBERTY, BUTTERSCOTCH

CODENAME : AGENT BEARBOT
SPECIAL SKILLS : 250 JIGGABYTE MEMORY,
64 TERRAHERTZ PROCESSOR,
EMBROIDERY
DISLIKES : COMPUTER VIRUSES
LIKES : FOLLOWING RULES, KITTENS

CODENAME : AGENT IRWIN
SPECIAL SKILLS : 24 LITRE ORAL STORAGE UNIT,
SLEEPING, EATING
DISLIKES : WORKING, BEING HUNGRY
LIKES : CHOCOLATE, CAKES, SAUSAGES, CRISPS, BURGERS,
PIZZAS, YORKSHIRE PUDDINGS, CHIPS... ER, DID I
ALREADY MENTION SAUSAGES?

CODENAME : AGENT REX
SPECIAL SKILLS : HELLO! WHAT AM I SUPPOSED
TO WRITE HERE? IS CUSTARD
A SPECIAL SKILL? HELLO?
DISLIKES : PARDON?
LIKES : CUSTARD

CODENAME : AGENT BEESLEY
SPECIAL SKILLS : GENTLEMANLY BEHAVIOUR,
QUEENSBURY RULES BOXING
TEA MAKING
DISLIKES : CADS, SCOUNDRELS, TOMFOOLERY
LIKES : A ROLLICKING GOOD ADVENTURE, WOT!

NOW THAT SOUNDS LIKE A SUPERB IDEA!

① START OFF BY DRAWING A SORT OF LUMPY BEAN SHAPE:

I SAY, I AM MOST CERTAINLY NOT 'LUMPY'!

② GIVE HIM SOME EYES AND A MAGNIFICENT MOUSTACHE:

NOW, THAT'S MORE LIKE IT.

DON'T FORGET THE MONOCLE!

③ ANY GOOD BEE HAS A FINE SET OF STRIPES AND A NICE SHARP STING:

OH YES, SPIFFING INDEED!

LOOK!

④ THEN ADD THE EARS AND TUSKS:

NOW SEE HERE, WHAT'S ALL THIS??

MAKE THE EARS REALLY BIG

⑤ OH SORRY, I MEAN ADD THE ANTENNAE, LEGS AND WINGS:

AH YES, THAT'S MORE THE MANNER OF THINGS!

OH, AND A LITTLE PIPE!

⑥ AND FINALLY, ADD THE DRESS AND BONNET:

THIS IS AN OUTRAGE!

I'LL HAVE YOUR HEAD, YOU SCOUNDREL!

AND THAT'S HOW YOU DRAW BEESLEY!

I HAVE AN URGENT MISSION FOR YOU, AGENTS! INVESTIGATE THESE OTHER TOP SECRET FILES FROM  LIBRARY AT ONCE!

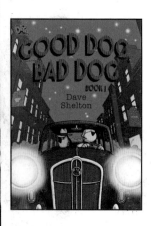

WE'RE ALL COUNTING ON YOU!